Southern Region

THE **CHANGING RAILWAY** SCENE

Southern Region

KEVIN ROBERTSON

Ian Allan PUBLISHING

Front cover: **This picture, taken in about August 1960, records the unusual sight of a Class L 4-4-0 No 31768 at Salisbury on a special working from Waterloo. At this time this was one of two members of the class still surviving, No 31768 was destined to be the final member of the class, in service until December 1961.**

Rear cover, top: **This is modern image, old and new style. An LCGB special with 6-PUL set No 3041 alongside a more modern 4-BEP unit No 7033 is seen against the buffers at Eastbourne.**

Rear cover, botton: **This is the 'Bournemouth Belle' behind 'West Country' class 4-6-2 No 34002** *Salisbury,* **although diverted from its usual route and recorded here passing Funtley, between Eastleigh and Fareham on 8 November 1964.**

Half-title page: **This is Swanage yard with Class M7 0-4-4T No 30667 seemingly paused during shunting operations whilst attached to a numbered set of BR Mk 1 coaches.** *D. Stribley*

Title page: **4-COR set No 3143 with a '91' headcode (fast service between Waterloo and Bournemouth) was recorded at Basingstoke.** *Tony Woodforth collection*

Below: **'Battle of Britain' class 4-6-2 No 34063** *229 Squadron* **demonstrates an everyday appearance when it is seen here outside Salisbury shed. This particular locomotive was never rebuilt and survived in service until 15 August 1965.**

First published 2009

ISBN 978 0 7110 3380 1

All rights reserved. No part of this book may be reproduced or transmitted in any form or by any means, electronic or mechanical, including photocopying, recording or by any information storage and retrieval system, without permission from the Publisher in writing.

© Ian Allan Publishing 2009

Published by Ian Allan Publishing

an imprint of Ian Allan Publishing Ltd, Hersham, Surrey KT12 4RG
Printed in England by Ian Allan Printing Ltd, Hersham, Surrey KT12 4RG

Code: 0907/B

Visit the Ian Allan Publishing website at www.ianallanpublishing.com

All images are from the Author's Collection unless otherwise shown.

Contents

Above: **Colour views from actual Southern Railway days are rare. Whilst Southern livery may still be seen today in museums and on preserved lines, the likelihood of a vast new archive of unseen pre-nationalisation colour images surfacing is probably remote. (Fortunately that has not been the case with the BR-Southern era). Consequently, the indulgence of the reader is requested for the first two views which are included for the benefit of historical importance. What is seen here is Class H16 4-6-2T No 516 fresh from overhaul at Eastleigh in April 1938 and sporting Maunsell livery. At this time this Locomotive was slightly less than 17 years old and had a further 22 years of service ahead.** *CCQ slides*

Below: **With the scarcity of colour film for the period, we can be grateful that any views were in fact recorded in the 1930s. Also, this was one where the image is not the conventional three-quarter scene of the time. Taken at Tunbridge Wells Central, it shows 'Schools' 4-4-0 class No 910 *Merchant Taylors* awaiting departure on what was clearly a wet day.**

Introduction

Change is a fact of life, sometimes welcome, sometimes resisted, but both are inevitable just the same.

Writing this in 2009, it is perhaps difficult to be objective when attempting to describe a changing railway scene over past decades. In any work, task, or profession, including the railway industry, change that has taken place has accelerated over the years. The regret is that often the intended fruits of previous change have not been allowed to prove their worth, or were considered too slow to take effect before a further alteration was commissioned.

The author has generalised the results up to now, with good reason. To any professional railwayman, some of the changes over the years will indeed have been welcomed with open arms. Those that have altered and improved working conditions, safety or of course wages and salaries, would have been approved. By dint of human nature, matters affecting the opposite or, equally important, were perceived to be detrimental, will likewise have been resisted. Sometimes of course this resulted in a withdrawal of labour – strike action.

The difficulty in attempting to record change objectively is to draw a distinction between genuine improvement and issues where a rose-tinted perspective is instead taken. Generalising again, the obvious example of this was the change over from steam as the principal motive power, although of course this was a change that been under way in various areas on the Southern since before 1923. Who could blame the men for preferring a clean, warm and dirt-free cab compared with the physical exertions necessary when working on steam? Maintenance facilities too were improved; no longer were almost the only tools available to the men a spanner, hammer, chisel and a bench vice. Anything else was achieved through brute force. Small wonder that with such primitive working conditions the relevant statutes, notably the Factories Acts, made specific exemptions to railway facilities. This was when nearly every depot was stuck fast in the 19th century let alone the 20th.

Into these conditions the railway industry was still attempting to both recruit and retain staff. It was far from easy. Higher wages and cleaner working conditions were available in almost every alternative employment and the drain of experienced and competent men was considerable. This then was also another reason why a railway management were forced to improve conditions and modernise. Whilst a genuine core of dedicated staff remained throughout, others were on the railway simply because it was a job, a means to earn a living. Who could blame them?

The other factor to consider harks back to the efficiency and modernisation changes taking place in every department. Jobs that existed for years were disappearing overnight. A classic example was signalmen. Here a man would have worked his way up from a booking lad or lad porter through, first, to a minor signalling post, probably on a branch line, thence through the grades until reaching a busy main line job. Overnight though that would change; he would be made redundant, having instead to apply all over again for one of a very few inside jobs at the new panel and possibly some miles further away. If you were successful, fine, if not it was perhaps a job on the platform pushing a brush, or at worse the dole. There are not many jobs outside for a skilled signalman, whilst the bitterness and resentment this occasioned also can be understood. We should not forget that a man can only take so much. There are cases where a person was made redundant, forced to take a lower grade task and be made redundant a second – perhaps even a third – time. Progress has costs, both human and financial.

Outside the industry though, the enthusiast continues to look at the railway through rose-tinted spectacles and, to be fair, that is indeed what now follows. Yes, it was sad when the products of Adams, Drummond, Urie, Maunsell and Bulleid, not forgetting Stroudley, Billington, Riddles, Jarvis and the like, were consigned for scrap, but such is the way of life throughout the centuries. The latest product of yesterday is cast aside and replaced by the newer model tomorrow.

Where this was such a tragedy is when vast sums had been expended and then in effect wasted. Equipment was not allowed to perform its intended task over its allocated time scale, purely due to a change in policy. The classic example here has to be with the steam locomotives of the BR Standard classes and likewise the members of the 'Bulleid' breed later rebuilt by Jarvis. Steam locomotives may be said to have a generally allotted lifespan of between 30 and 40 years, perhaps even this may be a little on the conservative side, but even taking the lowest figure, not one Standard or Bulleid locomotive achieved this. All of the latter type, bar one, were originally intended to have been consigned for scrap, to be recycled and to reappear as razor-blades, motor car components, or even girders and reinforcements used for construction. Think about it, the next time you drive in your car down a motorway. Most of these roads have been either built or certainly extended since the demise of steam. The very first bridge you pass under may include metal recycled from your favourite steam locomotive.

So the next question to be asked is, how did this change come about and, equally important, was it justified and was there even an alternative?

To answer these questions we need to delve back to the pre-war Southern Railway when, as an independent company, it had followed the lead given by what was probably one of the greatest contemporary General Managers of any British railway company, Sir Herbert Walker.

Walker had taken the lead in 1923, pursuing electrification as being the future not just for pure suburban services, but later for longer main line workings as well. In this respect it may be argued that he was simply following the obvious economic course. Whilst the embryonic LBSCR overhead system may have been preferable, the cost of extending this compared with the third rail was undoubtedly prohibitive. Even so, Walker was also correct in allowing the 'overhead' to continue in operation for some years. Fortunately, this was at a time when change was not considered necessary purely for change sake, or to attempt to quickly abolish the memory and influence of an absorbed company or organisation.

We should also consider for a moment the technological changes in engineering, in so far as reliable motive power was concerned. Go back to the 19th century, when railways were perceived as likely to go no further than a few short miles, serving little more than a local community. It was the bringing and linking together of numerous small systems that resulted in the equivalent of what is now referred to in aviation terms as 'a shrinking world'. Except of course then, instead of the world shrinking, it was a country that was shrinking. London to Brighton for example had once been considered a journey to be prepared for, considered, with bags and clothing taken for what would undoubtedly be an overnight stay. But, as trains became faster, so the requirement to consider this journey as other than as a day trip diminished. The result, and this point will be referred to in more detail later, was that instead of being seen as a main line, such a journey was now instead perceived as being little more than outer suburban.

Through its own devices, the Southern Railway quietly pursued this Outer Suburban theme, reaching out to bring the towns of the south coast into its extended suburban network. Eastbourne, Worthing, Chichester, Portsmouth and Alton would all follow; perhaps what is surprising is that Dover, Folkestone and Hastings (via Tonbridge) were excluded. The difference in mileage between say London and Dover at 75 miles, compared with the 50 miles between the capital and Brighton, somehow became all the more marked because for the latter locomotive-hauled coaches remained the norm at this time. Somehow a locomotive and coaches seemed to make all the difference.

With hindsight also, the Southern may have equally missed the opportunity to develop new routes and locations. That through Tolworth to Chessington was one of a very few where a new line was built to serve a new need. North of the Thames the example of 'Metroland' was not copied, in this Walker may have missed a chance.

Possibly though, the reason for this was simply that the vast amounts being spent on electrification meant there was little enough left for a dividend to the shareholders. Investors' needs had to be satisfied, so further investment needed to be attracted. There were undoubted opportunities that could have been taken and we shall never know all the ideas that were undoubtedly considered and rejected. One, however, may be of interest. This was the attempt made to introduce a form of Automatic Train Control, similar to the Hudd system, demonstrated to the LMS. Whilst this worked perfectly well, the Southern instead decided to invest in more modern signalling, feeling that the advantage of being able to run more trains to a closer headway and thereby achieve greater line occupancy was preferable to the need to cater for the occasional fog problems. In view of the generally good safety record of the SR, this was indeed perhaps the correct decision to be made at the time. Perhaps it serves also as an example of how with a limit to available funds there was a need to prioritise on what was consider to be the essential, compared with the desirable.

Perhaps this might even have been the reason why electrification in itself was pursued rather than the potential for new lines mentioned above.

On the motive power scene, the Southern had, as with the LMS and LNER, inherited a motley selection of machines. There had been some attempt at standardisation, but with the priority given to investment in electrification and likewise associated modern signalling, this meant that the requirements of steam were increasingly being neglected.

It would take a new man, the enigmatic Oliver Bulleid, to alter the thinking at Waterloo back towards steam. How he achieved this is all the more mysterious, bearing in mind the pre-existing statements made by the Southern that electrification was to be continued ever westwards. Southampton, Bournemouth, Salisbury and even Exeter were all intended to come into the third rail network.

Opposite top: **In this view of the Swanage branch taken on 15 August 1963, the ubiquitous 'M7' class locomotive, number unknown, is sandwiched between three coaches. Maunsell push-pull set No. 612 leads in the approach to what is unmistakably Corfe Castle. These sets were converted from 1959 onwards and were intended as replacements for the earlier units. As such, this was indeed representative of the changing Southern scene, a more modern, albeit converted vehicle. Their reign though would be short-lived, being replaced here by diesel electric units.**

Opposite bottom: **For a while during the 1930s and again in the 1950s, the 'Schools' class were utilised on through services to the Western Region via Oxford. For reasons that are not clear, both the Great Western and its successor, the Western Region, were never keen on the type working through on a regular basis and consequently the appearance of a 'Schools' at Oxford was unusual. This resistance by the Western is perhaps all the more surprising, bearing in mind the number of 4-4-0 type locomotives the GWR once possessed. (Was it even a throw back to the only outside cylinder 4-4-0 the GWR had, the original 'County' class and which were notoriously rough riding?) Here Class V 4-4-0 No 30930 *Radley* has arrived at Oxford from the south and waits to be detached.** *ADC slides*

But both the Southern Board's intentions and likewise those of Bulleid would end up being thwarted by events in Europe. We can only imagine what stage electrification would have reached under a continuing privately-owned Southern Railway, likewise a Bulleid Pacific with its originally intended Caprotti valve gear,

For the present however, we must now gloss over almost the whole of the period 1939-45 and instead look at the shape of the railway system subsequent to World War 2. This would indeed set the stage for the changes that were to take place in the 1950s and beyond.

What is known is that without doubt the Southern was in nowhere near as good a shape in 1945 as it had been in 1939. The reasons for this were obvious and will not be repeated here. Suffice to say that together with the GWR and LMS it was attempting bold steps towards regeneration, and to be fair it was also leading the field.

Further electrification was thus planned and indeed announced in 1946. This was all the more surprising, given a socialist government in power whose election manifesto included the nationalisation of the transport network and which therefore included the railways. (It is easy to forget that it was not just the railways that were nationalised; the waterways network, the docks, and a new creation British Road Services, as well as several omnibus operators, all came under the overall control of the British Transport Commission.)

But such a conglomerate needed time to settle and it was for this reason that very wisely the policies of the original owning companies were allowed to continue for some time to come. Whether it was in the event wise to continue to build Bulleid Pacifics almost non-stop for a further two years after 1948 will be open to debate for many years to come. Perhaps in reality it is a shame that the investment available was not directed at furthering the stated aims of the Southern towards modern traction. It has often been said that the electrification of the main line out of Euston in the 1960s was a wonderful achievement – but it should have taken place ten years earlier. The Southern had already laid the foundations for the expansion of their own electrification years earlier, at what cost then compared with numerous new steam locomotives?

It is expected that at this stage some readers will be shaking their heads in disapproval. But you cannot run a railway on sentiment. Today's preserved lines have learnt this to their cost; you need to adapt to survive. Hence the plethora of 'themed' days, aimed much more now at the family compared with the enthusiast. The same happened with the stage-coach owners of the 19th century; it does not matter what you produce, provide or offer, if nobody wants it. The railway network, whether in preservation or as a commercially-owned business, as is today, has to

provide what the customer requires. Possibly the latter statement is a bit tongue in cheek, as it seems every so often we have to continue to reinvent the wheel. The needs of the shareholders seem to have a priority over the very individuals, the customers (passengers) who are the bottom line for providing a shareholders' dividend in the first place. It is a lesson that is still being learnt over and over again and yet the answer is in effect simple; provide a better and more efficient service and there is benefit to both.

The difficulty in the 21st century is now that with set train formations only and loose stock no longer being available, an extra vehicle cannot be tagged on the end at times of need. Likewise, whereas in Victorian times the transport needs of an area were perhaps perceived as meaning there was a market in travel between point 'A' and point 'B', that may have altered over the years. In fact in most cases it probably has, but point 'C', which was ignored two hundred years ago, is nowadays perhaps equally important. Why, oh why, do we not simply respond? Modern traction can cope with gradients far steeper than years ago; the building of new railways is essential and should not be hampered by red tape.

At last though the author can now get off his soap box and return instead to the main intention of this narrative, to record the principal changes that have affected the Southern in the past five decades.

Aside from livery and title changes, there was really little to identify differences in the nationalised from the private railway in the immediate aftermath of nationalisation. To the rail enthusiast perhaps, the locomotive exchanges, which saw such scenes as a 'Royal Scot' and an 'A4' at Waterloo, were perhaps the most obvious features. Only a few years later of course, 'foreign' motive would again be working in and out of the terminus consequent upon the temporary withdrawal of the Bulleid designs with suspected axle flaws.

But away from the norm, the Southern was still continuing its innovative development programme. This was still fronted in the main by Bulleid, whose 'Leader', 'Tavern Cars' and 'Double Deck' units were all to be seen within 24 months of the network having passed to public ownership. That all three failed to achieve what had been intended is not to be discussed here. Suffice to say that there can be no advancement without experimentation. Whilst perhaps all three were intended to be seen as experimental, it must for ever be a matter of regret that the opportunity was not taken to develop further the ideas of a man who was in many ways a genius. It must be conceded though that in other areas the term flawed genius might be more appropriate.

Subsequent to the dust having settled, the Southern Region as it then was continued through to around 1955 with little change. More would occur in the following decade than in any equivalent time span in the history of either the Southern or its constituents. This had its origins in the 1955 Modernisation Plan, which affected not just the Southern Region but the whole of British Railways.

Subsequent to 1955 there was at last the opportunity to continue the aspirations of General Managers like Sir Herbert Walker and (later) Sir Eustace Missenden. Electrification to the Kent Coast was the first, continuing also with the third rail policy even though elsewhere on BR 25Kv AC overhead had been decreed as standard. (Interestingly, various overbridges which were necessarily reconstructed on the Southern Region, both before and subsequent to this date, were all given sufficient clearance for future overhead wires).

The new stock for the Kent Coast Electric services appeared around 1957 and before entering service some of these units were stored on the down line of the Ardingly branch. Nowadays such action would be deemed unthinkable – and not because the line is no more, but because of the likelihood of attention from graffiti artists and vandals. Fifty years ago however, it would appear that if there was any trouble it was limited.

Shortly before this, new diesel stock had also appeared on the Hastings line. Necessarily following a narrow width profile, the interiors were based on both compartment and open schemes, this still being the preferred form of travel. Later, the travelling public, instead of being consulted, would be told what they should like. Any apparent prior consultation and opinion was either ignored or manipulated into the design it had always been intended to produce in the first place. Both the electric and diesel-electric train sets mentioned were loosely based on the then standard Mk 1 coach design and were popular from the outset.

The difficulty came a few years later when further new stock was required to commence replacement for the PAN, PUL and COR sets of Southern Railway vintage. Rather than progress with the times and when the rest of British Railways was moving towards the Mk 2 coach design, the Southern Region engineers appeared constrained by earlier principles. Aside from a slight rounding of the ends, which would alter the external appearance somewhat, internally these were still Mk 1s. Even worse, though, was to follow. The 1967 Bournemouth electrification witnessed the centre vehicles for the TC and REP sets converted from locomotive-hauled Mk 1 steam stock, albeit on new bogies. They were noisy from the start, whilst any attempt at increasing ventilation with an open window resulted in a veritable hurricane within, thus making conversation almost impossible. Air conditioning for main line, or should it be outer-suburban trains, was still some years in the future.

Indeed for some time to come, and through to today, the Southern Region and its successors are likely to retain third rail electrification indefinitely. Meanwhile in the 1960s, coaching stock on trains from Waterloo and Victoria was relatively poor compared with that running out of Paddington, Euston and King's Cross.

At the same time as electrification took place in Kent, steam was being eclipsed on excursion traffic in the same area. A fleet of diesel-electric locomotives was on order for the Region and destined to be the D65xx series,

although as a stopgap until the first delivery some Sulzer Type 2 machines were loaned from the London Midland Region. The new D65xx machines would eventually form the mainstay of the SR diesel fleet for many years to come.

Of course, electrification did not extend to every branch line. Whilst plans were certainly made for its extension over routes like that through Steyning and also the Mid-Hants, steam for the present reigned supreme. But its days were numbered. Having proved the worth of the Hastings units, the same basic engine design was used in a fleet of two- and later three-car units built at Eastleigh for branch line duties across the Region. Steam could thus be ousted; where economies of scale were considered the better option, the alternative was closure.

The Southern Region would thus lose a considerable number of branch and cross-country routes this way; with hindsight one may wonder over the economics used to sanction some of these closures.

This though was the time of Dr Beeching. To be fair, if it had not been this man it would have been someone else. What is perhaps so sad is the way such wholesale closures and reductions were effected. Sometimes little in the way of consultation appears to have taken place. The men at Lancing for example, operating what was accepted as the most efficient carriage repair shop anywhere on BR, were condemned. Seemingly, this was on the basis of one flying visit by an axe-wielding representative from the Railways Board.

Possibly though, there were some closures which were at the time understandable. For a long time the majority of the former Southern lines to the coast beyond Salisbury and likewise the routes west of Exeter had been a problem for Waterloo. Certainly well patronised and profitable in the summer months, the remaining eight months of the year witnessed identical operating costs but limited revenue to cover these. Possibly some form of pruning was inevitable, but in the end the decision to transfer everything west of Salisbury to the Western

Opposite top: **This is the 'Bournemouth Belle' behind 'West Country' class 4-6-2 No 34002 *Salisbury,* although diverted from its usual route and recorded here passing Funtley, between Eastleigh and Fareham. Due to the route taken, the train will have to reverse at Fareham before setting off this time to run via Netley to Southampton. Such a performance would have been likely to have added around one hour to the schedule. It is 8 November 1964.**

Opposite bottom: **To be seen on the Southern Region in steam days were several of the BR Standard tender classes. These included 20 examples of the BR Class 5 4-6-0 type allocated to the Southern Region and given the names of, but not the original nameplates from, withdrawn 'King Arthur' class locomotives. This is No 73119 *Elaine* being watered at the west end of Platform 4 at Southampton Central. Alongside, another Standard of the smaller '76xxx' 2-6-0 type waits in the bay alongside. In the background is the view of the new docks, with the liner SS *United States* in the background. The view, whilst undated, was probably recorded in the early 1960s and whilst the steam locomotive, coaching stock and signals no longer survive, the liner still does. Sadly, however, she has been mothballed for many years at an American dockyard and despite several attempts at preservation, her future remains undecided.**

Above: **Literally at the end of steam, former 'King Arthur' class 4-6-0 No 30766, once named *Sir Geraint,* is being dismantled outside the rear of Eastleigh Works on 24 January 1959. Behind it is an Adams Class B4 0-4-0T No 30087, awaiting the same fate.**

Below: **After the Bournemouth electrification, the Southern Region relied heavily on Class 33s to operate main line passenger services on non-electrified lines. These were often on push-pull workings with 4-TC sets, Indeed this was often the method used on trains not passing beyond Salisbury, one such working being seen here with the locomotive leading.**

Region probably saved Waterloo from making an unpleasant choice. Paddington would instead take the blame. On economic grounds closure was justified, on social grounds that was never the case. An opportunity was lost. West of Exeter, the closure of the lines to Ilfracombe, Plymouth via Tavistock, Padstow and Bude, will for ever be regarded as a calamitous mistake.

Equally wrong was the seeming collusion between Regions to close the Somerset & Dorset. If ever a line would have benefited from more modern motive power allied to some obvious rationalisation, this was it. Sadly, after the last trains ran, there was an almost indecent haste to deliberately destroy the actual infrastructure, before it seems a subsequent management could have second thoughts about reinstating all or part of the route.

With electric and diesel traction now running hand-in-hand within Kent and likewise Sussex, the remainder of the Region, namely the Bournemouth and Salisbury lines, were bound to follow. Steam was finally abolished in July 1967, slightly later than had been intended, but the few extra months were occasioned by the new stock not being ready. Even so, it was a close run thing with several bigger diesels, members of the Brush Type 4 class, having to be borrowed to fill gaps in available motive power. There had even been requests that steam should continue beyond July 1967, but the run-down condition of the remaining fleet meant that this was just not possible.

It subsequently appeared that the Southern Region had in fact been offered front line redundant steam motive power from the LMR some years earlier, with examples from the 'Duchess' class and possibly even some 'Royal Scots'. For various reasons these were rejected, possibly because at the time the SR fleet was still considered sufficient. It was only with the prohibition of steam repairs that the situation really began to deteriorate. The repairs decision eventually had to be rescinded in 1966. Had it not been, there would have been an ever increasing number of gaps in the timetable from autumn 1966 onwards.

Meanwhile Salisbury became almost a dead-end as far as Waterloo was concerned. This was now the limit of Southern Region autonomy. Accordingly, the through services between Waterloo and Exeter were operated with Western Region motive power. WR 'Warship' diesels were now to be seen, although there was also no secret that Paddington regarded its own Exeter service via the Berks & Hants as being of greater importance than that between Waterloo and Exeter.

Subsequent to 1967 the situation, certainly for passenger services, was really one of entrenchment. A new electric or diesel railway existed. The majority of Southern Railway built stock was either already withdrawn or about to be disposed of, replaced by variants of the original CEP units dating back to the late 1950s. The ignominy of this was apparent when it was realised that locomotive-hauled stock on the various inter-regional services that penetrated the Southern Region was already to a better

standard. Just around the corner were the new Mk 3 vehicles, soon to be introduced, except on the Southern Region, as part of the HST sets. This variation was all too apparent to the passenger if an overall rail journey involved more than one Region's trains.

On the suburban network, the various SUB and EPB units held sway. Here the situation was more difficult; the need for maximum capacity in minimum space. Six-a-side compartment stock was thus still in considerable use in the 1970s, fine for the accountants in their offices, provided of course they were not forced to reach those same offices crammed in like sardines. Somewhere along the way, someone had ignored the fact that human beings come in a variety of shapes and sizes.

Moving away from passengers, a major change had also taken place for freight. In this area, wayside yards were almost extinct. The limited parcels traffic that remained was now invariably carried by passenger train, whilst in consequence redundant yard facilities were either sold off to developers or turned into additional car-parking facilities. Indeed, within a very short time, more revenue was being accrued from parking charges than had been achieved from freight, although with this change came further redundancies.

Additionally the major sorting and transfer yards, Nine Elms, Hither Green, Feltham, Eastleigh etc, were similarly rendered redundant. Some were quickly given over to a seemingly growing requirement for engineers' vehicles, whilst others were obliterated. Alternatively, they were found limited use as discharge points for bulk train loads, aggregate being the favoured commodity. One might even wonder where all this additional engineers' equipment had been previously stored? The railway may be contracting, but it seemingly had larger requirements in so far as track maintenance was required. The answer was simple; in past years maintenance had been concentrated over smaller areas, but now these numerous small depots no longer existed. These were the ones which had previously been the home to perhaps six or so men, one of whom would be required to 'walk the length' on a daily basis. Instead, staff were concentrated at set locations and travelled to and from their work site in a road lorry, which also provided messing requirements during the actual work phase. Thus the former SR concrete huts placed at intervals at the lineside were likewise redundant.

But with any progress to be made there are likewise lessons to be learnt. One terrible example was at Hither Green in 1967 when a broken rail, caused it was said by the heavy pounding of multiple-unit stock on track joints, resulted in derailment and death.

Progress here had meant track was no longer inspected on a daily basis, although fortunately engineers quickly realised deterioration increased far quicker as the speeds of multiple-unit stock increased. The regular passengers could have given the engineers this same information earlier. A Mk 1 coach, even with modern bogies, seemed to accentuate the problem. It was a hard lesson to learn.

Concurrent with the new trains and loss of freight was the installation of a more modern signalling system. Colour light MAS had first come to the Southern as far back as 1930, but its progress then stalled after 1939 and it was not until the 1960s that further expansion took place. By this time much of the semaphore signalling was already life-expired. It was an irony that men would talk of the opportunity MAS has given for faster train running, at a time when the actual level of service was less than it had been in mechanical days.

This though was hardly the fault of the Southern Region. Here it had to tow the party (BR) line. Traffic was welcome, provided it was regular, without the peaks associated with the past. This was the desired ideal. For this reason seasonal traffic, whilst not exactly discouraged, was hardly encouraged either.

The difficult economic times of the 1970s were hardly the fault of the railway itself. There was limited opportunity for investment from a government permanently it seemed strapped for cash. Indeed cost savings were still required; the result was that rolling stock now already due for replacement, or at least refurbishment, was forced to continue working. It was not the fault of the railway, but this was hardly appreciated by the passengers.

A change in the early 1980s witnessed a new direction taking place. It commenced with various forms of rebranding, then sectorisation. Twenty years later, this might even have been seen as an initial attempt at a future move towards privatisation, as was indeed the avowed intention of the government then in power.

But what the system needed more than investment in new paint and rebranding was wholesale investment in both the infrastructure and rolling stock. Both would indeed come, but it would take a change of owner, something inconceivable a decade earlier.

Meanwhile some tinkering did take place. The long-suffering Bournemouth line commuters were at last promised an improvement with the construction of five coach 'Wessex' electric sets, although as ever, the slogan 'We're getting there' was wearing somewhat thin. A more accurate analogy was perhaps that the proverbial light at the end of tunnel never appeared to be getting any closer.

The end of the Southern Region would come about not because of a further change of boundaries, but instead due to revisions in preparation for privatisation. The form this would take was at that time controversial and indeed remains so to this day. Instead of particular areas being sold off, the right to operate services on certain routes was considered the way forward, with the actual track network sold to another separate organisation. All would, to some degree, remain under varying forms of government control.

The success, or otherwise, of the now privatised network is beyond the scope of the present work and the author leaves it to others to dissect the subsequent changes that have taken place. One improvement at least was some much needed new rolling stock, although whether this is responsible for what has been a rapid increase in passenger numbers or if the latter is due to people simply becoming totally fed up with ever increasing road congestion, is a mute point.

Sir Herbert Walker might not have approved, but somehow perhaps the author thinks that Oliver Bulleid would. After all, he may be said to have been the one man on the old Southern not to have been afraid of 'blue sky thinking'.

Below: **BRC&W Type 3 No D6506 is recorded at London Bridge on a Dover service in 1961, having just passed Southwark Cathedral. This was a slightly unusual working for a member of the class, but the operating authorities were keen to see how the type would perform on a variety of duties.**

1

Tank Locomotive Scenes

Top: The survey proper of the changing Southern scene starts with examples of the steam locomotives running in the British Railways period; the electrics will come later. Of the steam stock inherited by BR, in 1951 this included 12 Stirling Class R1 0-6-0Ts of the South Eastern Railway, represented here by No 31047 with No 31128 behind. In front it is just possible to glimpse part of a third member of the class, No 31010 This was one of the type fitted with a short chimney and rounded cab, enabling it to work on the Whitstable branch. *ADC slides*

Above: Far from its original haunts on the former 'Brighton' system, here is Class E4 0-6-2T No 32473 on an empty stock working at Waterloo. The 1950s witnessed a variety of locomotives on this type of duty, which for many years had been the sole preserve of former LSWR designs and particularly the Class M7 type. Pilot locomotives were still required when steam was superseded by diesel on the Waterloo–Exeter services, although with multiple-unit operation now the norm, like the steam locomotive, the pilot is no more. In this view, notice may be taken of what appears to be the Fireman wandering back towards the locomotive, having evidently filled the tea can. It is 30 April 1962.

Above: **Without doubt the most well known of all the former Brighton steam tank classes must be the 'Terriers'. Their light weight guaranteed their longevity to enable them to work locations such as the Shoreham Harbour and Hayling branches where nothing larger was permitted. This particular example, Class A1X 0-6-0T No 32640 is recorded at what is probably Fratton, its diminutive size exemplified by comparison with the coal heap alongside. No 32640 was already 85 years of age when photographed in March 1963, but was withdrawn from service with British Railways later in the same year. After initial static preservation at a Butlin's holiday camp, it has now found a permanent home on the Isle of Wight Steam Railway as W11, which number was carried when working on the Island system between 1930 and 1946.**

Left: **This is a 'Terrier' in action. The view is taken from the first coach of a Hayling Island train shortly after leaving Havant. This branch succumbed to closure in 1963, ostensibly due to the condition of the wooden viaduct over Langstone Harbour but probably equally likely because the 'Terriers' were almost life-expired and the cost of upgrading the line was prohibitive. The branch was thus destined to be one of many lines to cease operation under the old 'Southern Region' rather than be part of a changing scene.**

Above: **The buffer stops at the Hayling Island terminus; any further and the route would have been on the beach! Class A1X 0-6-0T No 32646 has disgorged the passengers from its train, who are seen making their way out of the station. The locomotive has run forward preparatory to running round and returning to Havant. The date is 26 August 1963.**

Below: **Like the 'Terriers', the LSWR Class O2 0-4-4Ts on the Isle of Wight were equally well photographed. This was partly because of their own long lives, but also because the Island lines remained a steam stronghold until the end. The changing scene on the Island would mean not just modernisation and the replacement of steam by more modern motive power, but instead a complete revolution in the infrastructure as well. But that is another story. Before that took place, here is Class O2 No W30 *Shorwell* in the up platform at Ryde St Johns Road and with another, unidentified, member of the class behind the fence.** *M. Radford*

Above: **Adams 'Radial' 4-4-2T Class 0415 No 30582 returned to its former haunts at Windsor & Eton Riverside on a special working on 19 March 1961. To be fair, it would have been many decades since an locomotive of this type had worked the steam suburban service between Waterloo and Windsor. The three survivors were about to be considered obsolete from their former duties on the Lyme Regis branch. They migrated to Eastleigh, where they were used for a while on enthusiast workings.**

Below: **An even older class of LSWR tank locomotives than the Adams 'Radials' that survived into the 1960s were the three 2-4-0WT Beattie well tanks. These formerly worked the Wenford Bridge branch. Class 0298 Nos 30585, 30586, and 30587 are all seen at Eastleigh having made the long, and no doubt slow, journey from Cornwall to Hampshire for the last time. As with the Adams 'Radials', the Beattie tanks were used on several special workings around this time.** *M. Radford*

Top: **A clean example of the LSWR 'M7' class is seen here in the form of push-pull fitted 0-4-4T No 30031. Certainly unusual, possibly even unique, was the provision of wording above the various air pipes on the buffer beam, although to be fair this may have been present on other push-pull members of the class and simply obscured by dirt. Behind are two other members of the class although certainly not in such pristine condition. The view was of course taken at Eastleigh.**

Above: **Within the Hampshire area, the push-pull fitted members of the 'M7' class found employment on several branch lines, including for many years the Brockenhurst–Lymington shuttle. Also, at times the stock used would not facilitate push-pull working, such as here with the now preserved 0-4-4T No 30053 at Lymington Town on a three-coach service to Brockenhurst.**

Top: **It is almost the end of an era for the 'M7' class on the Lymington service. The date is March 1964, with the M7s destined to be replaced by Ivatt and Standard tank locomotives on conventional steam workings. This particular locomotive is 0-4-4T No 30052, recorded on the down journey to Lymington.**

Above: **Class M7 0-4-4T No 30052 recedes into the distance with a Brockenhurst–Lymington push-pull working in March 1964.**

Bottom: **The driver in his compartment takes the single line tablet for the section to Lymington Town from the signalman at Lymington Junction where the branch leaves the main line. Push-pull set No 384 was formed in June 1948 and comprised two LSWR vehicles, Nos 3212 and 6563. Originally working the Bentley to Bordon service, the coaches were later employed on Lymington trains until both vehicles were withdrawn in December 1962.**

Above: **Besides the Lymington service, a second one using push-pull stock and an 'M7' class tank from Brockenhurst was that serving the 'old road' via Ringwood. This is seen with 0-4-4T No 30107 propelling a Ringwood service, the eventual destination of which will be Bournemouth West. This particular set, No 662, was of former SECR vehicles and likewise lasted until December 1962. The date is 27 December 1960.**

Below: **In the late summer of 9 September 1961, Class M7 0-4-4T No 30031 has charge of the 10.45 am Broadstone to Brockenhurst working near Lymington Junction and thus close to its final destination.**

Above: **Running on the main line approaching Sway, Class M7 0-4-4T No 30110 is at the head of a three-coach Bulleid set, No 828, on 9 September 1961.**

Below: **Close to Lymington Junction, the camera has recorded the 4.17pm Brockenhurst to Bournemouth West with set No 385 being propelled by an unrecorded member of the 'M7' class. It is 8 July 1961 and these former LSWR vehicles would last little more than a further year.**

Above: **This impressive low angle view is of Class M7 0-4-4T No 30111 in charge of the 11.40 am Brockenhurst to Bournemouth via Ringwood service on Boxing Day 1961. This particular locomotive was one of a handful of the 'M7' class to remain active into 1964, although to be fair the condition of all the members of the class was by now very poor. This particular line too would never see a diesel service, being closed in May 1964.**

Below: **This is what would nowadays be referred to as a 'shuttle service' although 40-odd years ago such words were hardly in the vocabulary. Class M7 0-4-4T No 30056 is propelling the 2.05pm Brockenhurst to Bournemouth West working on the last part of its hour-long journey, seen near to Parkstone on 18 August 1962.**

Above: **Class M7 0-4-4T No 30107 was in charge in this view taken at Bournemouth West. The date is not recorded, but of course must be relatively early in the BR era as witness the red livery. Set No 2 was of former LSWR vehicles and had formerly seen service on the Meon Valley line before graduating further west.**

Below: **It must not be forgotten that the push-pull fitted members of the 'M7' class worked in the Guildford area, notably on services through to Horsham via Baynards. This is indeed the route headcode displayed on 0-4-4T No 30051, seen here taking water at Guildford on 18 June 1960.**

2
Tender types

Top: **Three examples of the tender locomotives of the Southern are seen here with Class C 0-6-0 No 31690 at the head. (Behind is a Class U Mogul 2-6-0 No 31797 followed by a 'Schools'). The location is Ashford shed, recorded during the late summer of 1961. Together with two sister locomotives, No 31690 was used at this time mainly as one of the works' shunters at Ashford.**

Above: **Sporting a goodly load of coal, another member of the Class C 0-6-0 No 31510 is recorded on the turntable at Bricklayers Arms on 8 April 1962. Despite seeming to be in reasonable external condition, this locomotive was withdrawn just two months later, a victim of progress whereby there was little work remaining for it to perform.**
Meteor Film Services

Above: Arguably the best known of all the Ashford-built locomotives, certainly in later years, were the Mogul classes. Members of the 'U' and 'N' classes were active until the mid-1960s, although as would be expected this was in ever decreasing numbers. Here Class U 2-6-0 No 31801 arrives at Basingstoke with a down Salisbury line stopping service. Originally built as a 'K' class tank *River Darenth* (the actual river rises in Kent and is a tributary of the Thames), the locomotive was rebuilt in the form seen here in 1928 and lasted in service as a tender varient until June 1964. *Tony Woodforth collection*

Right: This is a slightly unusual scene of a former Brighton Class K 2-6-0 No 32337 on a passenger working in Hampshire. The occasion was a summer extra from Portsmouth on 14 August 1959. This may well have been an extra working at short notice, as there was nothing shown in advance within the weekly Special Traffic Notices. The train is seen here near Bitterne and displays a Salisbury destination headcode although this was no guarantee that the working would actually continue beyond Southampton.

Below: This picture, taken in about August 1960, records the unusual sight of a Class L 4-4-0 No 31768 at Salisbury on a special working from Waterloo. The train is heading west and has just passed Salisbury West signalbox. The low pressure pneumatic point motor will also be noted in the 'six-foot'. At this time this was one of two members of the class still surviving, No 31768 was destined to be the final member of the class, in service until December 1961. It was subsequently broken up at Eastleigh.

Above and below: These two views are of '700' class 0-6-0 No 30339 at Cannon Street on 18 September 1960 with the first leg of the LCGB 'South Western Ltd' tour. This particular locomotive was in charge from Cannon Street to Ascot, running via Ludgate Hill. The tour eventually made its way via Alton, Eastleigh, Fawley and Broadstone to Templecombe before the run back to Waterloo. With the exception of an S&D 2-8-0 for the Broadstone–Templecombe–Salisbury leg, former LSWR steam classes were used throughout.

Top: **Class H15 4-6-0 No 30523 is seen at the head of what may well be a stopping service to Waterloo or even a summer relief. The location is Bournemouth Central, which would retain its two centre tracks until rationalisation occurred consequent upon electrification in 1967.**

Above: **On a Basingstoke to Bournemouth working, 'King Arthur' class 4-6-0 No 30788 *Sir Urre of the Mount* is seen near Lymington Junction on the main line via Sway on 9 September 1961. This was the last summer of service for this locomotive, as together with the remaining members of the class, all were withdrawn during 1962.**

Above: **A member of the Class S15 4-6-0s No 30832 is working well as it heads south past Battledown on a down Bournemouth line passenger working. The placing of only one headcode disc was probably simply because there was not another one available.** *Tony Woodforth collection*

Right: **The Class S15 4-6-0s were the mainstay of heavy goods workings on the Southern for many years. Whilst older of course compared to Mr Bulleid's Class Q1, they possessed an advantage in that the braking characteristics of locomotive and tender were far superior when in charge of an unfitted train. The type would also find themselves pressed into service on occasions for passenger working, such as here with a special from Waterloo to Reading. No 30839 is seen at what is thought to be the 'Midhurst Belle' tour of 18 October 1965.**

Below **'Schools' Class V 4-4-0 No 30905** *Tonbridge* **is shown in steam at Clapham Junction. The locomotive is attached to the class's solitary self-trimming tender which was transferred from No 30932** *Blundells* **to run with No 30905 in August 1958 having been incorrectly painted green by Ashford Works. No 30932 itself having been repainted black.**

Top: **Class S15 4-6-0 No 30499 rushes through Raynes Park on the down fast line with what could well be empty stock, all of which would appear to be BR Mk 1 type.** *D. Stribley*

Above: **This is a close look at the 'Schools' class, the withdrawal of the last of which at the end of 1962 was caused as much by a lack of further** suitable work as well as being in need of repair. Regardless of where they were recorded, the class will forever be associated with the narrow loading gauge of the Hastings line, which of course necessitated the distinctive cab profile. Seen here is Class V 4-4-0 No 30912 *Downside*, complete with a 'Lord Nelson' bogie tender, powering through Vauxhall with a boat train for Lymington Pier on 14 August 1961.

Above: **In the background is the imposing entrance to the now closed Dover Marine on 9 September 1961. We tend to recall filthy locomotives a few years later, notably Bulleid Pacifics of course, but here is 'Schools' Class V 4-4-0 No 30915 *Brighton* in deplorable condition. Somewhere underneath, there was supposed to be a smart green livery. Mechanically the locomotive must have been sound as this was one of the class to remain in service until the end and was withdrawn in December 1962.**

Below: **This view of a 'Schools' portrays Class V 4-4-0 No 30935 *Sevenoaks*, ostensibly still operational but certainly not in as good an external condition as Class D1 4-4-0 No 31487 behind it. The view may have been taken at Gillingham sometime in 1960.** *ADC slides*

Top: **This is the end of the road for Class S15 4-6-0 No 30840 at Eastleigh, on 2 February 1965. No 30840 had completed 28 years of service, but was rusting away having been withdrawn in September of the previous year. Interestingly, this was one of the five members of the type (the others were Nos 30838/39/41, 42) that were prohibited from working passenger trains on the Eastern Section, whilst similarly being restricted to 45mph.**

Above: **Slightly unusual and certainly not cost effective, 'Lord Nelson' class 4-6-0 No 30853 *Sir Richard Grenville* runs east past Lymington Junction towards Brockenhurst and presumably Eastleigh. It is 28 August 1959.**

3
The Bulleid Breed, 'Q1' and Light Pacifics

Above: **This is a summer special on the Lymington branch. The unmistakable outline of a Class Q1 0-6-0, in this case No 33020, is near the site of the former Shirley Holmes Halt. It is in charge of the 3.30pm Waterloo service on 27 August 1960. It would be very unlikely that the 'Q1' would have taken the train all the way to London and instead an locomotive change possibly took place at Brockenhurst.**

Below: **In its original form, 'West Country' class 4-6-2 No 34097 *Holsworthy* is recorded in charge of the 9.40am Brighton to Bournemouth train at Lymington Junction just west of Brockenhurst on 28 March 1959. This locomotive was one of several members of the class based at Brighton and used on the through coastway services. It was withdrawn for rebuilding in 1961 and lasted in service until April 1966.**

Above: This wonderful portrait of 'Battle of Britain' class 4-6-2 No 34051 *Winston Churchill* is ex-works at Eastleigh. Despite the gloss finish, the effect of the light shows the result that years of service have had on what was a previously smooth casing. *M. Radford*

Below: This view is of 'Battle of Britain' class 4-6-2 No 34051 *Winston Churchill* on its famous duty at the head of the funeral train of its illustrious namesake. It was this duty which confirmed the locomotive for preservation and to represent the Bulleid 'Pacific' type as part of the national collection. *ADC Slides*

Above: **On a visit to the Swanage branch, 'West Country' Class 4-6-2 No 34007 *Wadebridge* arrives at the terminus on a featherweight service. Possibly this was a fill in turn for the locomotive, although it may also have been through coaches from Waterloo.** *M. Stribley*

Right: **Head on at the buffer stops at Swanage, the lady passenger has a seemingly passing interest in the locomotive. The use of a 'Pacific' is all the more surprising given the background, leafless trees, obvious steam escaping and the passenger wearing an overcoat, all pointing to the winter period. Was the appearance of 'West Country' class 4-6-2 No 34007 *Wadebridge* even a replacement for a failure?** *M. Stribley*

Above left: Seen from the bank alongside the station, 'West Country' class 4-6-2 No 34007 *Wadebridge* is clearly generating more steam than was required at the time, whilst the seemingly full tender makes it ever more likely this was indeed a rushed replacement for the branch line locomotive. *M. Stribley*

Above right: From an angle not usually recorded, this is the easternmost down platform at Bournemouth Central. Due to its length, the down platform was split in two with a crossover mid-way. This was one of the reasons that the former through lines were useful. 'Battle of Britain' class 4-6-2 No 34073 *249 Squadron* will probably now proceed to Bournemouth West.

Below: The double-headed 4.43pm from Ilfracombe service is seen here crossing the River Taw on the outskirts of Barnstaple with Class N 2-6-0 No 31833 piloting 'West Country' class 4-6-2 No 34033 *Chard*. Neither could be said to be a good reflection of their respective classes. It is 22 May 1961.

Above: A Bulleid 'Battle of Britain' class Light Pacific No 34055 *Fighter Pilot* is seen east of Woking with a lightweight Salisbury line working. The signals here are to pure Southern Railway design, reflecting the decision made by the SR in the 1930s to invest in colour light technology rather than ATC on the basis of being able to increase line occupancy. *M. Stribley*

Below: 'West Country' class 4-6-2 No 34038 *Lynton* was photographed west of Brockenhurst in the New Forest at Lymington Junction with the 9.30am Waterloo to Bournemouth working on 3 June 1963. This particular locomotivee spent part of its final years of service as a regular performer on the rerouted 'Pines Express', working turn-and-turn about with sister engine 'West Country' class 4-6-2 No 34102 *Lapford.*

Top: **Against a background of its decidedly shabby comrades, 'West Country' class 4-6-2 No 34019 *Bideford* presents an impressive sight at the rear of Eastleigh shed. The rust on the 'Standard' alongside is all too obvious. Although undated, the view may well have been taken around September 1963, which was the occasion of the locomotive's last repaint. Several minor works visits still followed, the last being in the autumn of 1966. No 34019 was finally withdrawn in March 1967. It would not survive the cutters' torch.**

Above: **This totally different location can be clearly identified as at the foot of the cliffs between Folkestone and Dover. This is 'Battle of Britain' class 4-6-2 No 34064 *Fighter Command*, running light and displaying the correct route headcode.**

Opposite top: **The penultimate member of the 'Light Pacific' type, 'Battle of Britain' class 4-6-2 No 34109 *Sir Trafford Leigh-Mallory* is entering Bournemouth Central from the west. Rebuilt in 1961, this locomotive had only three years in service after this and was withdrawn and cut up in 1964.**

Opposite centre: **Running past Barton Mill carriage sidings east of Basingstoke, 'Battle of Britain' class 4-6-2 No 34062 *17 Squadron* is in charge of an up west of England working, the lead vehicle of which is an LNER full-brake. During the steam era the sidings here were invariably full of locomotive-hauled stock but were subsequently electrified and now form a stabling point for the EMUs of the modern railway.**

Opposite bottom: **Coming down the bank from Battledown Flyover and routed by the local line at Worting Junction, 'West Country' class 4-6-2 No 34047 *Callington* has charge of an inter-regional working. Despite this being a prestige service, the routeing of the train onto the local line at this point was fully justified. Shortly after this, at Basingstoke itself, the line to Reading will involve taking the curve to the left and so by being on the local line, the main line is left unobstructed for other services.**

Above: At Basingstoke, 'Battle of Britain' class 4-6-2 No 34085 *501 Squadron* awaits departure for Reading and Oxford with the 'Pines Express'. After Basingstoke, these locomotive-hauled trains invariably called at Reading West only, a local service following to take any passengers from the West to the General station at Reading. No 34085 would return south later in the day; some of the 'Light Pacifics' heading north on the inter-regional trains were scheduled to take a down freight via Newbury.

Below: This diverted working is of 'West Country' class 4-6-2 No 34034 *Honiton* on the 9.56 am Weymouth to Waterloo service running through Netley on the line towards Fareham. A reversal at Netley may have been required, although the alternative was to continue east before taking the Portsmouth Direct line through Petersfield and Guildford to finally regain the usual route at Woking. The date is 10 October 1965. Twenty years after the Bournemouth electrification, this route as well as that via Botley were electrified.

Opposite top: This is one of the 'Merchant Navy' 4-6-2 types, represented here in original form by No 35026 *Lamport & Holt Line* passing through Bromley South. The presence of the coach roof boards would imply that this was a prestige working and destined for either Folkestone or Dover. *Pursey Short*

Opposite bottom: Attracting the admiring attention of photographers, 'Merchant Navy' class 4-6-2 No 35014 *Nederland Line* may well be just about to leave Platform 3 at Basingstoke bound for the Bournemouth line. In the left background are the remains of the GWR terminus, the site of which is currently being considered for one or possibly two through freight lines leading directly onto the Reading route and so avoiding congestion at the passenger station. *Tony Woodforth collection*

4
'Merchant Navy' class

Above: A grimy and travel stained example of the 'Merchant Navy' class 4-6-2 No 35022 *Holland-America Line* seen alongside the walls of the 'new', 1910, Nine Elms shed early in 1965. This locomotive would survive into 1967 and sent to Woodham's Barry scrapyard. Rescued for preservation there are currently no plans for it to be restored.

Below: This member of the class is at least temporarily out of service. 'Merchant Navy' class 4-6-2 No 35002 *Union Castle* is hemmed in by wagons at Bricklayers Arms depot in 1961. It is possible that the it was awaiting spares and had been shunted as seen to leave the remainder of the depot as clear as possible. No 35002 was indeed reinstated to traffic although it was taken out of service some time before the final demise of Southern steam.

Above: **On 10 February 1964, the down 'Bournemouth Belle' was in charge of 'Merchant Navy' class 4-6-2 No 35027 *Port Line*, recorded here just west of Wimbledon at the point where the suburban line to Sutton diverges. It is passing a 4-SUB suburban unit on the up slow line to Waterloo. Pullman was not a word considered to have a place in the swish electric railway that was to be the Southern Region after 1967 and like the steam locomotive this train was consigned to history.**

Below: **Back in service and complete with headboard, 'Merchant Navy' class 4-6-2 No 35022 *Holland-America Line* storms through Basingstoke non-stop with the up 'Atlantic Coast Express'. In the background is the locomotive shed playing host to a BR Standard and a WR Mogul.** *Tony Woodforth collection*

5
Standard Types, BR and LMR, on the Southern

Above: **Standard Class 4 2-6-4T No 80152 is seen here at Reading Southern on what could be a Redhill service. The locomotive was then based at that depot and so could be working an out-and-back duty. Always the poor relation in the town, the former Southern station at Reading was rendered redundant in 1965 when a pair of additional platforms was added at Reading General with services then diverted over a short new spur line. The former Southern site has since been redeveloped.** *Tony Woodforth collection*

Left: **In the days when snow did fall in January, this is a bitterly cold day at Bricklayers Arms depot on 2 January 1962. A Standard Class 4 2-6-4 tank, No 80145 whose home shed was at Brighton, is recorded being serviced alongside what appears to be one of the coaches from the breakdown-train. The Southern Region had a number of these modern tank locomotives, several of which were built at Brighton and were utilised mainly on the Central and Western sections.**

Above: **Here Standard Class 4 2-6-4T No 80152 is seen at Oxted in company with an Class H 0-4-4T No 31518. The Standard Class 4 tank locomotives were often used on the important commuter services between Victoria and Oxted and in the case of any delays were the subject of regular complaints.**

Right: **This location for Standard Class 4 2-6-4T No 80152 is not recorded. The signals certainly imply a junction with what is an electrified route, although it is tempting to suggest from the look of the first vehicle that the working may well have been a branch service.**

Below: **Smaller in size than the Standard Class 4s but equally modern were the Ivatt Class 2 2-6-2T design. A number of these were likewise based on the Southern Region from late 1951 onwards. (This may have been a direct result of the type having been at Bath, S&D shed, where they evidently earned a good reputation.) Originally examples of the class were seen on all three divisions but as electrification advanced they slowly migrated west. This included a short spell on the Lyme Regis branch, before services there ceased. Here No 41292 is recorded running around its train at the Dorset terminus in preparation for the return trip to Axminster.**

Above: In the West Country an unidentified Ivatt Class 2 arrives from Bere Alston and enters the terminus at Callington in August 1961. Fortunately, this is a branch of which part still survives although trains no longer reach Callington. It is though possible to travel over a section of the former Plymouth, Devonport & South Western route from Bere Alston as far as Gunnislake.

Below: There are no longer trains of any type to Sidmouth, once served from the appropriately named Sidmouth Junction on the West of England main line. On 20 August 1961, this was the scene at the branch terminus where a Standard Class 3, 82xxx series 2-6-2 tank locomotive waits with the branch train in the yard. Passenger workings on the branch ended in March 1967.

Top: **Just along the coast from Sidmouth was the terminus at Exmouth and where once trains from both Tipton St Johns and Exeter would arrive. Today it is only the latter route which is in use, Standard Class 3 2-6-2T No 82013 is arriving from Exeter Central with the branch service, a journey which would have taken around 25 minutes for the 10¼ miles inclusive of four or five stops.**

Above: **An Ivatt Class 2 2-6-2T is seen here on the Swanage branch. These capable locomotives had replaced the 'M7' class on these workings. No 41312 is leaving Corfe Castle for Wareham with the 3.05pm service from Swanage on 27 August 1966.**

Above: The BR Class 3 2-6-2T locomotives were designed at Swindon and extended to a total of 45. Again as a replacement for the Class M7s at Waterloo, the 2-6-2Ts found employment on empty coaching stock duties in and out of the terminus. No 82014 is seen between such duties in May 1964.

Left: From the vantage point of a train near Ringwood hauled by a Standard class tender locomotive, there is just a glimpse of one of the crossing keeper's cottages on what was known as the Castleman's Corkscrew. The original Southampton & Dorchester railway was referred to as such due to its tortuous route west. It was for this reason that a more direct connection to Bournemouth was built from Brockenhurst onwards, the line between Brockenhurst and Broadstone, which included Ringwood, but this was subsequently abandoned. This was one route on which diesel traction was never operated. In Ringwood as well as elsewhere on the course of the old railway, the line's traces have largely been obliterated. *Tony Woodforth collection*

Below: Typical of the services on the Wimborne/Ringwood line in its final years were those hauled by BR Standard Class 4 2-6-0 locomotives in the 76xxx series. This scene is of No 76027, unusually with a Maunsell push-pull set in tow. This may have been a stand in for an 'M7' class duty.

Above: **Possibly standing in for a failed 'Pacific', a Standard Class 4 4-6-0 from the 75xxx series hurries east through the New Forest with an up Waterloo train from Bournemouth. The Southern Region was also not adverse to 'borrowing' a locomotive which might have arrived on a through working from another Region, or using one for a bit longer than was strictly necessary when on a running in turn following repair. Consequently it was not unknown for Stanier Class 5s to appear on Waterloo services although the more unusual workings have included an '8F' and Caprotti-fitted Class 5.**

Below: **Awaiting its next turn of duty at Basingstoke shed, Standard Class 5 4-6-0 No 73065 stands in the afternoon sunshine. The Southern Region had around 30 members of the class allocated for much of the 1950s although the actual locomotives varied over the years.**
Tony Woodforth collection

6
Interlopers and Specials

Above: **Running down the gradient past the closed goods yard at Shawford, Stanier Class 5 4-6-0 No 45493 has charge of the 10.08 York to Poole The siding leading to the goods yard at Shawford had been taken out of use as early as July 1951 although, as can be seen, the building was still standing some years later. The yard site was subsequently taken over by a civil engineering company.**

Below: **Class T9 4-4-0 No 30117 is seen at Portsmouth Harbour on 30 April 1961 whilst at the head of the Fareham leg of the LCGB 'Solent Ltd' tour. This outing involved no less than six different steam locomotives commencing from Waterloo and then travelling via Portsmouth, Fareham, Droxford, Gosport, Netley, Southampton, Southampton Docks, Eastleigh Works, Newbury, Reading, Ascot and finally back to Waterloo. On the left is 4-COR unit No 3057.** *M. Stribley*

Above: **A rail tour and clearly on S&D metals at Bailey Gate, Somerset & Dorset Class 7F 2-8-0 No 53804 is working the Broadstone–Templecombe–Salisbury leg of the LCGB 'South Western Ltd' trip of 18 September 1960.** *M. Stribley*

Below: **Special workings were not always popular with the operating authorities, as witness the 'enthusiast' seemingly having just taken his photograph from off the platform. The locomotive is of course one of the unmistakable 'USA' class 0-6-0 tanks No 30073 and is recorded in Platform 3 at Eastleigh. Possibly, it is about to take the 30 April 1961 tour south to Southampton Docks via the nearby works.** *M. Stribley*

Above: **Perhaps working the first leg of the Southampton Docks tour of 30 April 1961, 'Lord Nelson' class 4-6-0 No 30856 *Lord St Vincent* is seen at Waterloo. This was the year that withdrawal of the class commenced, six having been taken out of service by December. The remainder, including No 30856, had also been laid aside by the end of 1962.** *M. Stribley*

Below: **The only Class S15 4-6-0 to remain operational into 1966, No 30837 was one of the last three operational members of the type, which were withdrawn in September 1965. No 30837 was however retained for special workings; whether it did any revenue-earning turns at this time is unknown. It was certainly in use for what was almost the last time on 9 January 1966, near Alresford with the 'S15 commemorative tour'. (One further special with the same locomotive took place a week later.)**

Above: **The slightly incongruous combination of the surviving Adams Class T3 No 563 in company with a 1957 design electric locomotive is seen inside Eastleigh Works in 1961. Sixty years separates the two designs; the 'T3' is in the process of being 'conserved' prior to exhibition at Clapham Museum. The steam locomotive had been restored to LSWR livery back in 1948 but had deteriorated badly over the years. Eastleigh was now removing the tell-tale signs of years of neglect after which it was painted in a pink undercoat, with the topcoat subsequently applied at Clapham.** *M. Stribley*

Below: **For a while from 1962 onwards, Class T9 4-4-0 No 30120, now running as LSWR No 120, was employed on a variety of special workings. At least eight of these were recorded in the following 18 months. The decision had already been made that this example of the class would be preserved as part of the national collection and consequently it was withdrawn for storage. In more recent times No 30120 has been seen on a number of preserved lines and likewise in either BR black or Southern green livery as No 120.**

7

The Changing Scene –
the End of an Era

Above: An example of the end of steam, Standard Class 4 2-6-4 tank No 80019 is seen between Lymington Pier and Lymington Town attached to a Mk1 coach in the then latest BR livery. The locomotive still seems in good external condition and may well have been attended to by 'volunteer' cleaners. It certainly compares well with the filthy condition of the 'Bulleid' Pacifics running on the main line around this time, **1966/67.** *Tony Woodforth collection*

Below: The look at the steam motive power of the Southern Region concludes with a few shed and works views. This of course is Eastleigh, late in the day for steam, on 7 May 1966. The locomotives are the unrebuilt 'West Country' class 4-6-2 No 34102 *Lapford* and the rebuilt No 34040 *Crewkerne*. Both would remain active until the very end of steam in July 1967, after which, and like the depot here, they would be consigned to the history books.

Top: The rear of Eastleigh is seen here and this time with not a single example of an SR design visible. The date is not given but is likely to have been around the mid-1960s. At the time the shed also played host to a visiting 'Caprotti' fitted Stanier Class 5 4-6-0, seen at the head of the line up nearest the camera. The locomotive on the extreme right is Standard Class 4 2-6-4T No 80137, with Ivatt Class 2 2-6-2T No 41294 immediately behind. Above the locomotives is the office block and water tank, whilst nearer is the coal stage. The roof of the works can also be seen against the skyline.

Above: This tender first line up is outside of the 'old' shed at Nine Elms on 14 August 1961. The products of both Ashford and Eastleigh can be identified, several also displaying the warning sign for overhead electric wires although there were of course but a few locations on the Southern system where overhead cables was a danger.

Below: A shed to survive to the end of Southern steam was Bournemouth, recorded here probably around 1960/61 with a goodly complement of steam power visible. That nearest the camera is Class M7 0-4-4T No 30112. The depot had evolved in the form seen here from 1938 onwards and replaced an 'ad-hoc' arrangement dating back to LSWR days. Even so, it was not ideal; the facilities were cramped, as was invariably the case where a shed was located close to a growing town. Here was also the famous notice requesting locomotives to be kept quiet as it was considered to be in the midst of a residential area. No doubt there were several relieved expressions when steam finally ceased working, the site being cleared soon afterwards.

Above: **The clutter associated with a steam works is typified here in what is believed to be a 1960 view of Eastleigh Works. 'Battle of Britain' class 4-6-2 No 34079** *141 Squadron* **is in the process of a light repair although this is the only locomotive that can be positively identified.**

Left: **The date is August 1966 and although steam repairs are still taking place at Eastleigh Works, they are of a very limited nature. The man with the cutter's torch is probably about to remove a somewhat stubborn fitting from a '76xxx' class 2-6-0. Immediately beyond it is a tender-less 'West Country' 4-6-2 No 34023** *Blackmoor Vale.* **The priority now is to keep the remaining fleet operational, with the minimum of maintenance until the replacement electric sets are ready.**

Below: **As the 1960s progressed, so the number of steam types being withdrawn and not replaced increased. These withdrawals were partly due to age and economics, but other causes were when the work once performed was no longer available. This might be due to line closures, or even the withdrawal of freight facilities. The 'M7' class were rendered redundant for all of these reasons. No 30047 was one of the earlier members of the class to be taken out of service in February 1960. It was then partly cannibalised with its motor gear transferred to a surviving member of the class, No 30133. No 30047 is seen here prior to being stripped and scrapped at Eastleigh on 27 February 1960.**

Above: 'Battle of Britain' Pacific No 34067, formerly carrying the name *Tangmere*, heads up the line on the scrap/works road at Eastleigh on 7 November 1964 and almost a year after it had been withdrawn. Evidently there must have been difficulty in removing the name plate and badge as the latter has been taken off with a flame torch. No 34067 would also give up its original tender at this time, which it is believed later ran behind 'West Country' No 34020 *Seaton*.

Below: Redundant 'W' class 2-6-4 tank locomotives are seen at Feltham in early 1965. The class had been rendered operationally extinct when No 31912 ceased working in August 1964. It then joined this melancholy line of two other members of the type and a solitary 'Standard' Class 4 2-6-4T awaiting the call to the scrap yard. In the distance a Class S15 4-6-0 no doubt awaits a similar fate.

8
Around the Region

Above: In this next section, the emphasis changes from looking at locomotives to looking at scenes. These commence with the Folkestone Harbour Branch. This short line diverged at Folkestone East Junction and thence via a gradient as steep as 1:36 continued down to the Harbour itself. It was used by main line services until quite recent years, at one time requiring several banking locomotives to assist a train returning to the main line.

Above: In typical Southern green, this is the informative sign at Dunton Green on the former SECR main line through Sevonoaks. As the sign also implies, this was once the junction for the Westerham branch, on which service ceased at the end of October 1961.

Below: The terminus at Hawkhurst is viewed looking towards the buffers. Services on this nine-mile branch from Paddock Wood ceased in June 1961, the intermediate stations of Horsmonden, Goudhurst and Cranbrook closing at the same time. The line had been open for slightly less than 68 years.

Above: Often associated with railway yards were large warehouses, their proximity occasioned by being able to receive supplies in bulk by rail. This is the former Scats (Southern Counties Agricultural Trading Services) warehouse at Alresford, photographed in 1970 and at a time when it was still very much in use although by now receiving supplies by road. In the foreground is the station car park.

Below: This 1970 view of Alresford shows how deserted the station actually was between trains. Today, of course, it is the bustling headquarters of the Mid-Hants Railway although sadly trains go in one direction only, towards Alton. The section south through Itchen Abbas to Winchester was abandoned at the time of closure by BR in 1973.

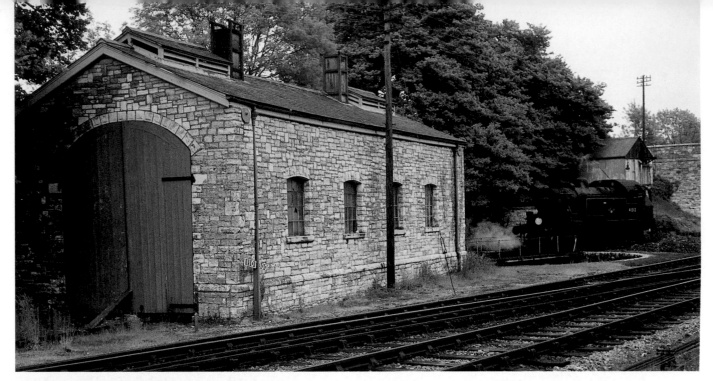

Above: The Swanage branch closed in 1972, the year before the Mid-Hants. Like the latter, it had witnessed a diesel service in its final years, although this had been insufficient to stave off closure. The neat shed was constructed out of locally quarried stone and was evidently still in use as late as June 1965, when Ivatt 2-6-2T No 41312 was availing itself of the servicing facilities.

Left: As with the locomotive shed, the station buildings at Swanage were also constructed from local material with, at the shore end of the station, this informative timetable. It made for easy reading by passengers and has been referred to as a Benni Cronin board.

Below: It appears as if the watering facilities and turntable at Swanage were probably the more used items. Years earlier there is photographic evidence, only in black and white unfortunately, of S&D liveried 4-4-0s being serviced at the shed having worked through services from Bath. The final years of the line saw nothing as dramatic and instead a shuttle service only was provided between here and Wareham.

Above: **The imposing frontage of Lymington Town station is seen in the evening sun of 6 June 1965. This is the only surviving coastal Hampshire branch line to carry passenger services and was electrified in 1966/67. In the 21st century the service is maintained with what are described as 'Heritage' CIG electric units but which were of the latest type in 1967. The remaining staff are also very proud of their railway, providing a personal service to 'customers' that would be impossible at larger centres.**

Below: **The Hayling Island branch was one of the coastal lines that did not survive to be either dieselised or electrified. The thought perhaps of a third-rail to Hayling does conjure up various images! Instead, we see the terminus of the branch which was still handling freight right up to closure in 1963. Indeed, up to that time the branch had probably been the final location in the country where mixed trains remained a feature of the timetable.**

Above: **The rural charm is that of Verwood, first station north on the line from West Moors to Salisbury via Fordingbridge. The view is of a southbound service, which will call next at West Moors and then all stations to Bournemouth West. The service is running 'wrong road', the signalling arranged so that trains from either direction would use the one platform with the section then from West Moors through to Fordingbridge.**

Left: **This correctly coloured station name board is at Fordingbridge. Workings through here ceased in May 1964, again without ever being dieselised.**

Below: **A route which did see a diesel service for a while was that from Andover to Romsey and through the picturesque landscape of the Test Valley. At Mottisfont, the first station north from Romsey, there was the curious arrangement whereby the station buildings were located at the end of the platform. This was said to be caused by subsidence, as witness the platform itself. The view is from an Andover-bound train.**
Tony Woodforth collection

Above: A local 'Hampshire' DEMU set has just departed north from Stockbridge towards Fullerton and Andover with all signals 'off' in both directions. Here, as at Verwood on the Fordingbridge line, the signalbox would spend long periods switched out of circuit. This meant a consequent reduction in staff costs, although against this was the restriction in line capacity. *Tony Woodforth collection*

Below: This view of Stockbridge is of the tile hung main building, and is perhaps not too appealing. The bases of the canopy supports have been recently daubed with white paint, although the rest of the timber and metalwork has evidently not been attended to for some time. The view is from the road bridge carrying what was then the A30 over the railway. Since closure, all signs of the station have been obliterated, along with the overbridge.
Tony Woodforth collection

Top: **Gunnislake was on the route towards Callington. This is the old station, now abandoned; the railway still serves the town but from a new site slightly east of the original. A DMU shuttle service is provided from Plymouth, which has to reverse direction at Bere Alston.**
Tony Woodforth collection

Above: **This shows the complex at Barnstaple Junction with the lines to Torrington, left, and Ilfracombe to the right. Here also trains would**

arrive from the Great Western route from Taunton. Rationalisation started here as far back as 1960 with the closure of the Victoria Road to South Loop Junction connection. It was followed by the closure of the Torrington line to passenger services, after which the line from Taunton ceased operation in 1966. Finally, the line to Ilfracombe succumbed in 1970, leaving the station a shadow of its former self and having now just a shuttle service from Exeter/Exmouth. China clay trains continued to run on the Torrington line until 5 March 1983.

Top: **Duplication of routes between the former GWR and LSWR meant that rationalisation was inevitable in places. One example was at Launceston where the GW had arrived from Lydford and the LSWR from Halwill Junction. Regretfully neither route was destined to be secure and after a brief foray with single car diesel units on at least the Halwill to Padstow service, that from Plymouth via Lydford ended in 1962. Services on the LSWR route ran until 1966.** *M. Radford*

Above: **Recorded during the final year of operation at Bude, this view was taken in the summer of 1966 and records a melancholy scene. Already the lines leading to the Quay are rusty and out of use, while the signalbox will soon be the haunt of vandals.** *M. Radford*

Left: Older facilities can be turned over to a new use. This former oil/gas lamp holder at Salisbury has been converted to electricity. The loudspeakers, in an instantly recognisable Southern style, will also be noted. *Tony Woodforth collection*

Below: A common feature during the 1960s and coinciding with the demise of steam was the considerable amount of track rationalisation that took place. One example is seen here, at Andover, recorded in the summer of 1966 from the front of a Western Region DMU of the type then operating between Reading and Salisbury via Basingstoke. (For a while these same units had a turn between Basingstoke and Waterloo as well.) This view is looking east. The down through line has already been curtailed into a siding, a fate that will later affect the up through line as well. Beyond the station, the bracket signal formerly had an arm allowing access to the line through Andover Town to Stockbridge and Romsey, although services here had ceased in September 1964. *Tony Woodforth collection*

Opposite top: East of Andover, there were stopping places at Hurstbourne and Whitchurch before arriving at Overton, seen here. Famous for serving the factory that for many years produced the paper on which bank notes were printed, the facilities here were slowly rationalised from 1965 onwards. Subsequent to 1970, all that was left were the up and down running lines, seen here. The view is looking towards Basingstoke. *Tony Woodforth collection*

Opposite centre: This is the outskirts of Basingstoke, showing a former LSWR coach demoted to departmental use. In the background are steam examples of BR, GWR and SR origin, whilst the modern white building was for years the headquarters of the firm Eli Lilly. *Tony Woodforth collection*

Opposite bottom: This is Winchfield, old style, taken in the summer of 1966 and the last months of operation in this form. Shortly afterwards MAS signalling was introduced, indeed it is just possible to see the new structures both near the gantry and also in the distance. At the same time, the final sidings were taken out of use although new sidings were provided as a temporary facility in 1970. This was to unload aggregate in connection with the building of the nearby M3 motorway. *Tony Woodforth collection*

9
Signalling and Infrastructure

Above: **Co-acting signal arms, necessary when a clear view was otherwise obstructed, were a feature of the steam age railway at a variety of locations. This is Botley, once the junction for the short branch to Bishops Waltham, although more recently a terminal for roadstone brought by rail from the Mendip quarries. The station building, dating back to the 1840s, was demolished in connection with the 'modern' railway. Its replacement is a bus-shelter type structure.**

Below: **A veritable forest of semaphore signals at the west end of Fareham station is seen in 1955. To the left is the line to Southampton via Netley whilst straight ahead was that towards Eastleigh via Botley and available through one of two separate routes. One of these was the 'diversion', a double-track connection avoiding the single bore of Fareham tunnel, whilst to the right the original tunnel line was used for services bound for the Meon Valley branch and Alton.** *S. C. Townroe*

Above: The original Southampton & Dorchester railway was required to provide for numerous foot and road crossings along its route westwards. In consequence, something in the order 43 lodges were provided on a route of some 55 miles. Each was numbered, this being No 7, east of Brockenhurst, which guarded a public foot crossing until superseded by a footbridge in June 1957. The building though continued to be occupied for some time afterwards, this view being taken from the replacement footbridge in November 1964. The cottage was finally demolished in 1978.

Below: On the type of duty for which the design was intended, Class S15 4-6-0 No 30505 is on a Nine Elms to Southampton freight working. The location is Otterbourne, between Shawford and Eastleigh. The train is likely to pull into the yard at Eastleigh to be re-formed. Services such as these continued to run after steam ceased, although they were eventually curtailed as yards closed and workings of fully-fitted block trains became the norm. It is 9 May 1960.

Above: A number of rural lines continued to be operated for freight traffic long after passenger services has ceased running. One of these was from Pulborough through to Midhurst, with intermediate stops at Fittleworth, Petworth seen here, and Selham. Passenger services had ceased back in 1955, although goods lingered on at Midhurst until 1964 and as far as Petworth until 1966.

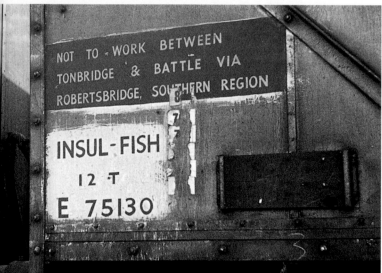

Left: This branding on an 'Insul-Fish' wagon shows the clearance restrictions on the Hastings line, a reminder that these applied to all forms of rolling stock. This was No E75130, one of the fleet of 'Blue Spot' fish vans which were designed for relatively high speed work on the East Coast Main Line.

Below: This scene was typical of many yards in the mid-1960s, freight having ceased and the facilities instead given over to storing condemned stock. This is the former GWR yard at Basingstoke, now devoid of revenue-earning traffic. In the background is a 4VEP set on the main line to Waterloo, with a DEMU also visible on the Basingstoke to Reading shuttle. *Tony Woodforth collection*

Above: Stored stock is seen in the west yard at Basingstoke and this includes one of the distinctive Southern bogie brake vans whose origins may be traced back to conversions of former LBSCR stock. This was one of the batch of Southern-built vehicles from 1936, the sides of which have also been partly covered in steel sheet.

Below: The conspicuous backdrop at Corfe Castle is seen against a Pullman 'Holiday Coach' in the siding. The vehicle is believed to be P43, formerly named *Coral*, an 8-wheeled Pullman Car dating from November 1921. This was in use at the station between 1960 and 1967. It is seen here on 15 August 1963 at the height of the holiday season.

Above: The Southern's renowned use of concrete is depicted here with the footbridge alongside the level crossing at Andover Town station. The signalman was often subject to abuse from road users due to the seemingly long wait necessary before a train would arrive. The design of the signalbox is to LSWR format. *Tony Woodforth collection*

Below: Local material has been used here at Swanage as the base for the signalbox. The actual box contained a frame of 23 levers, four levers of which had a 'push or pull' feature. The box closed in June 1967; there are conflicting dates as regards exactly when, although subsequent to this services were operated by DEMU sets on a single platform line. The odd special that did venture after this date had of necessity to be 'top and tailed'. *M. Stribley*

Above: **This was Millbrook, a large box on a main line and one of the standard Southern 'greenhouse' structures. A few still survive in use in the 21st century. This particular example dated from 1935, when four lines were provided between Southampton and Millbrook. The box remained in use until signal operation in the area was taken over by Eastleigh panel in 1981.**

Right: **Inside Millbrook box, the standard three-position Southern block instruments and repeaters were provided, and were still a feature of the box up to the time of closure. The more modern BR release plunger and black plastic point indicator will also be noted.**

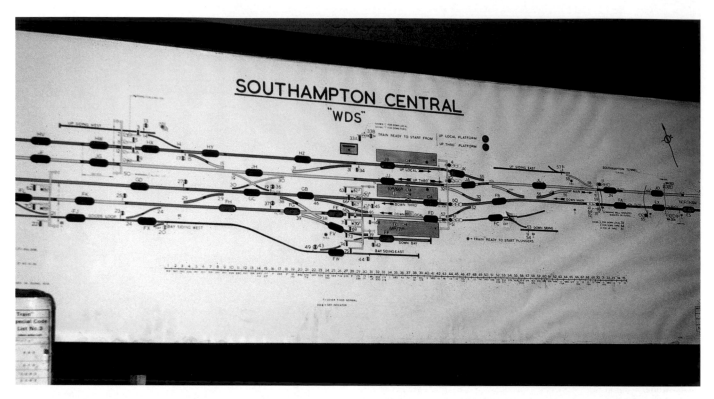

Above: **The illuminated diagram at Southampton Central, which contained a frame of 75 levers, was similar in design but not identical to Millbrook. From the diagram, the presence of four trains is apparent, one on the down main having just left the station, one on the up main, Platform 1 (top), another stationary in the Platform 5 bay, and finally one just appearing from the east and about to enter the 528 yard Southampton Tunnel.**

Below left: **The uniquely tall signalbox at Wimborne was designed and constructed to allow the signalman a view of trains arriving and**

departing from the west. Curiously, despite this view dating from some time in the early 1960s, the support column on the opposite platform furthest from the camera appears to be freshly painted in wartime blackout colours. Was there perhaps limited lighting here, even as late as this? *Tony Woodforth collection*

Below right: **This is a study in concentration. The view is inside the Southern Region signal works at Wimbledon, where even in the 1980s repairs were being carried out to equipment from the mechanical era.**

Above: **It is transition time and Dunbridge signalbox dating from LSWR days is shown with a modern level crossing with full lifting barriers.**

Right: **Modern signalling? Well, it was modern at the time. This is the original 'entry-exit' panel at Eastleigh, overlooking the main lines and yard. As a result of Eastleigh taking over a greater geographical area, including the Southampton complex, a new panel in an extended power box was opened later on the same site.**

Below: **This is Botley in 1978, showing a new use for an old structure. Although no longer used for signalling, the former box is now an office facility for the regular stone traffic arriving at the site. In connection with this traffic, the former bay platform once used by trains on the long-defunct Bishops Waltham branch also found a new use as a headshunt, whilst trains back onto the truncated branch line itself to offload their contents. The MAS signalling can be seen, with the roadstone terminal in the distance.**

10
The Unexpected and Unwelcome

Above: **Engineering difficulties are not associated with any particular era, one example being the embankment slip that occurred near Christchurch in early 1966. The track can be seen suspended over a void, with remedial work at an early stage. It took six months for full restoration to take place, during which time single line working was in operation at restricted speeds over the up line.**

Left: **Seen from track level, the extent of the Christchurch slip of 1966 is apparent, the rails literally left hanging. How the defect was noticed is not known, although fortunately it was discovered prior to a train attempting to traverse the gap.**

Opposite top: **A location where a major slip occurred, disrupting traffic, was between Hook and Winchfield, east of Basingstoke. This was on what was fortunately a four track section, with both the up local and up through lines affected. All traffic was now funnelled onto just a single line in either direction, the former down through route being converted into a temporary up line for the duration.** *Tony Woodforth collection*

Opposite bottom: **Seen from a passing train, this is a London-bound service moving from the up through line onto the formation of the down through route during the slip between Hook and Winchfield.** *Tony Woodforth collection*

11
Building a New Railway

Opposite page: **This is an overhead view of Permanent Way materials in general and sleeper stacks in particular at the former Redbridge civil engineering works, west of Southampton.**

Top: **The BR era witnessed a gradual move away from short 60ft rail sections to pre-stressed lengths of cwr – continuous welded rail. The preparation of this was a task undertaken at Redbridge for many years. This is a general view of what was referred to as No 1 Shop.**

Above: **New ballast is being added subsequent to the relaying of the up main line at Worting Junction, west of Basingstoke, in March 1976. The stone could well have originated from Meldon Quarry, near Okehampton. The dust associated with this work is obvious and this was also a problem when wagon loads of ballast were being transported.**
Tony Woodforth collection

12
A New Era

Top: **This is modern image, old and new style. An LCGB special with 6-PUL set No 3041 alongside a more modern 4-BEP unit No 7033 is seen against the buffers at Eastbourne. On its own, the sign offering Luncheons suggests that this was a year or two ago.**

Above: **The replacement for steam on the Basingstoke–Waterloo service was not necessarily luxurious. Where once locomotive-hauled corridor stock was used, the 1960s witnessed certain services being given over to 2-HAP suburban units. An unidentified set is seen leaving Basingstoke shortly after the third rail was energised in 1966.**
Tony Woodforth collection

Above: As part of the Kent Coast Electrification scheme, 24 Bo-Bo 2,552hp electric locomotives were provided for the Southern Region from 1957/58 onwards. Built at Doncaster, they were also fitted with a roof pantograph to be used in sidings where an overhead contact wire was provided in place of what would have been a hazardous third rail. Here the very first of the breed No E5000 is being inspected whilst brand new at Durnsford Road in 1958.

Below: No E5005 passes through Tonbridge on an old-fashioned freight, probably around 1960. Whilst perfectly suitable for this type of work, it was in reality hardly what the class had been intended for; the presence of the full brake immediately next to the locomotive implying this may well have been some form of test working. *S. Blencowe*

Above: **In pristine condition, Bo-Bo No E5015 awaits departure from Victoria with the down 'Golden Arrow' service. The green livery suited these locomotives well, although like any livery it was obviously best if kept clean.**

Below: **In definitely work-stained condition, an unidentified electric locomotive of the Doncaster build powers the 'Golden Arrow' service through Kent. At this time the train was still formed predominantly of Pullman stock, although as time passed the complement would reduce until there were little more than two Pullman vehicles.**

Top: A line up of three members of what later became Class 71 is seen at Hither Green depot on 19 October 1963. Nos E5002, E5003, and E5021 are present and the roof pantograph position is clearly visible.

Above: This summer 1966 view is of the front of Eastleigh Works, where an unidentified member of Class 71, seemingly repainted in blue livery and with a yellow warning panel, peers out from the workshop. The former locomotive works was now in the process of taking over repair and maintenance of the electric multiple unit rolling stock based on the Southern Region, in which role it would continue for almost a further 40 years.

Above: One of the first outings for new BRC&W Co built Type 3 diesel locomotives, No D6500, is recorded at Hither Green. These locomotives would form the mainstay of the Southern Region main line diesel fleet for many years, working both passenger and goods duties through the length and breath of the Region. They later became TOPS Class 33.

Below: This is BRC&W Type 3 No D6506. This class of 98 locomotives later became Class 33s, 12 of which were built to the narrower Hastings line gauge and 18 of which were later fitted with push-pull apparatus for operating passenger services west of Bournemouth.

Top: **Class 33 No D6540 is seen on 20 July 1963 in the smart original livery of a very pale grey waist band and window surrounds, with a Brunswick green body. Both are set off by red buffer beams.**

Above: **This slightly unusual combination shows BRC&W Type 3 No D6507 with Standard Class 4 2-6-4T No 80019 together running light between Swanage and Corfe Castle on 27 August 1966. The circumstances of this trip were not reported. A failure perhaps?**

Above: The BRC&W Type 3 D65xx series, later known as 'Cromptons', were equally at home on all but the very fastest and heaviest workings. No D6578 was recorded near Lymington Junction in charge of an eastbound freight on 5 June 1963.

Left: This photograph is included here because of the interest factor. BRC&W Type 3 No D6535 had failed at an unknown location and was being propelled to repair at Eastleigh by an 0-6-0 diesel shunter, just visible behind.

Below: To replace steam on the non-electrified branch lines, several series of diesel units were constructed at Eastleigh using generators and electric transmission. The design was based upon the main line 'Hastings' sets, with the exterior of the driving trailers also similar in style to contemporary EMU types. Here a DEMU set awaits departure from the waterside terminus at Fawley, 17 May 1965. Passenger services here were withdrawn the following year.

Below: Whilst bringing a touch of modern traction to the lines they worked, the visibility for passengers in the Southern DEMUs was no different from that gained by travelling in an ordinary coach. Hence it needed the curvature of the line to afford any advantage. This scene was taken from a three-car set on an Andover-bound service near Horsebridge, a route that would be closed shortly afterwards.
Tony Woodforth collection

Bottom: Two-car 'Hampshire' 2H unit No 1122 is seen on an Alton service, having just left Southampton Terminus and being recorded at Chapel Crossing. By the late 1960s, only three of the 'Hampshire' units remained as two-car sets, Nos 1120-1122, the remainder having had a centre trailer added. Known as 'Thumpers', they developed quite a following in their later life. Their withdrawal was hastened by their being slam-door stock, possible asbestos content and problems with their cast iron engine blocks which became porous over the years.
Tony Woodforth collection

Above: The hoped for salvation on the lightly used rural branch lines was the railbus. AC Cars No W79977 is seen at Boscarne Junction in July 1964. The operating costs of units such as this were still too great to afford a salvation for several lines, although the idea of steps affording access other than at stations was both novel and effective. However, passengers did need to be reasonably able-bodied to make use of this facility.

Left: This is an example of the rationalisation of the 1960s and is the workman's halt at Meldon Quarry near Okehampton. The route from Okehampton south had been reduced to a single track, with the 'stop' signal planted on the former position of the up line. It is July 1966. *M. Radford*

Opposite page: The unrestricted view from the WR diesel units operating the remaining services on the former Southern lines west of Exeter was welcomed by passengers. This train has just left Okehampton station. *M. Radford*

Above: For much of the system west of Exeter, rationalisation was not enough. This is the trackbed leading up the crossing of Little Petherick Creek near Padstow. At the time the photo was taken the bridge was closed off for maintenance, but has since been reinstated as part of a pedestrian and cycle route linking Padstow with Bodmin. *Tony Woodforth collection*

Left: At Eastleigh, where once lines of locomotives would stand either awaiting works attention or resplendent in fresh paint, there is instead concrete hardstanding and new offices. (More administrators, it seems, are necessary for less work.) Even the old liveried BR road vehicle looks singularly out of place.

Below: Rationalisation took place at Exeter Central. The former through roads have been removed or reduced in status, whilst the carriage shed now stands trackless. *Tony Woodforth collection*

Top: **An unidentified Brush Type 4, later Class 47, heads west from Basingstoke, probably destined for Eastleigh and then Fawley. No doubt the tank cars themselves on this bulk movement were running empty.** *Tony Woodforth collection*

Above **This picture shows the new order at Exmouth, a route that survives but only in so far as its connection to Exeter is concerned. In the bland all-over Rail Blue livery, a Western Region diesel-mechanical** set awaits departure on what is now regarded as a basic railway, devoid of all but non-essential facilities and fittings. *Tony Woodforth collection*

Below: **The unusual sight of 4-COR set No 3143 with a '91' headcode (fast service between Waterloo and Bournemouth) was recorded at Basingstoke. It is not clear if this was actually a lay-over for the set or a genuine duty for a Portsmouth line unit.** *Tony Woodforth collection*

Opposite top: A number of the former E50xx series of electric locomotives were converted in electro-diesel traction in consequence of the Bournemouth electrification, which work also involved the removal of the roof pantograph. In their new role they were intended mainly for duty on parcels and Southampton Docks workings, but their eventual sphere of operation was limited as the work for which they had been rebuilt disappeared rapidly. They were given a Class 74 designation and E6104 is seen passing Basingstoke with a Weymouth Quay-Waterloo boat train. The locomotive appears to be fresh from overhaul. *Tony Woodforth collection*

Opposite bottom: The interior of Bournemouth, once Bournemouth Central, became bland after electrification. Standing in the up platform are two 4-VEP sets, displaying their original all-over blue livery. At the time this was the limit of electrification other than for depot access, although the third-rail has since been extended further west to Weymouth. *Tony Woodforth collection*

Above: For almost 40 years after the end of steam, Eastleigh was the main maintenance depot for the fleet of electric units operating on the Southern. However, the building of new stock here had long since ceased. At the rear of the works where once boilers had been stocked and locomotives also cut up, there was now a traverser, serving several sidings, on which vehicles either newly reconditioned, awaiting attention, or stored were held. This view is of a newly reconditioned 4CIG electric unit No 7419 on the left keeping company with two former 'Hastings' unit coaches, the latter unlikely to run again.

Below: '93' was the headcode used for the stopping services on the Bournemouth line out of Waterloo, with 4-VEP set No 7711 seen here arriving at Basingstoke on a down working. The acceleration of these units was considerable; one evening turn saw two such units with a Class 33 on the rear between Waterloo and as far as Basingstoke, at which point the train would divide. The front four-car electric set would then continue to Eastleigh with the locomotive propelling the rear four cars as a stopping service to Salisbury. With the locomotive under power throughout, this was a service renowned as a definite 'flyer'.

Above: A fast combination was an unidentified 4-REP unit of 3,200hp (at the rear and in all blue livery) attached to the leading single 4-TC set No 407 in blue amd grey. This formation is seen here at Worting Junction where the West of England and Bournemouth lines separate, on a semi-fast Bournemouth line working. *Tony Woodforth collection*

Below: Even the new order later became dated. As replacements for the REP+TC sets, BR produced the Class 442 'Wessex' units, five-car sets incorporating certain components from the older stock. Once problems with the power door opening had been resolved, these sets provided almost 20 years of wonderful service, and were appreciated for the their quiet and smooth performance. Sadly, in the privatised era they were deemed 'non-standard' and despite having years of life ahead and popular with the travelling public, all were withdrawn prematurely. A new use has been found for some of these sets on the Brighton line, thus not allowing them to fall into disrepair as has happened in the past with other assets no longer required. *Brian Morrison*